Memory Verse Mysteries

Grades 4-6

By
Linda Standke

Cover Illustration by
Jack Snider

Inside Illustrations by
Julie Anderson

Carson-Dellosa Christian Publishing

Scripture taken from the HOLY BIBLE: NEW INTERNATIONAL VERSION®. NIV®. Copyright © 1973, 1978, 1984 by International Bible Society. Used by permission of Zondervan Bible Publishers.

The "NIV" and "New International Version" trademarks are registered in the United States Patent and Trademark Office by International Bible Society.

Credits:
Author: Linda Standke
Cover Illustration: Jack Snider
Inside Illustrations: Julie Anderson
Project Director: Sherrill B. Flora
Editors: D'Arlyn Marks, Sharon Thompson
Graphic Layout: Gray House Graphics

Printed in the USA • All Rights Reserved

ISBN: 0-88724-799-7

Table of Contents

Friendship
John 15:13

John writes that you cannot have a greater love than being willing to give up your life for a friend.

Begin with the ✚ row. Start with the number 3. Go down to the letter in the grid that matches the number. Write this letter in the first blank space below. Continue with the ♡, †, and the ⚱ rows to complete the verse.

✚	3	7	1	10	12	9	5	15	2	13	14	6	11	4	8
♡	1	9	10	5	6	7	15	2	14	12	13	8	4	3	11
†	15	8	2	6	10	14	4	5	7	1	11	3	12	13	9
⚱	6	11	5	13	8	4	3	7	12	15	2	1	9	14	10

1	O	B	E	U	L	A	A	L	N	T	E	U	S	T
2	T	R	E	R	O	L	S	N	O	R	I	L	O	V	E
3	G	S	T	S	V	L	I	H	O	P	E	I	R	H	W
4	N	R	B	D	E	H	D	T	O	C	M	Y	T	S	V
5	R	A	F	E	R	L	R	O	O	H	R	I	S	T	X
6	F	C	E	L	T	O	M	T	O	R	N	H	R	H	Y
7	P	R	F	A	L	H	O	S	W	I	B	R	S	A	Z
8	O	H	E	L	R	S	T	B	S	L	S	T	S	N
9	M	O	G	T	O	E	T	H	L	T	E	S	N	L	I
10	Z	L	N	A	A	L	P	E	E	B	S	U	B	O	S
11	O	E	H	I	H	O	E	E	S	E	H	W	A	V	A
12	P	N	I	G	T	R	O	Y	F	H	R	X	S	E	A
13	Y	P	J	O	M	D	P	O	S	V	I	M	I	L	R
14	X	T	K	T	O	Y	L	U	T	D	E	Y	S	D	E
15	T	W	L	H	S	M	A	L	E	R	P	E	A	C	E

" __ __ __ __ __ __   __ __ __   __ __ __   __ __   __ __ __

__ __ __ __   __ __ __ __ ,   __ __ __   __ __ __   __ __ __ __

__ __ __   __ __ __ __ __   __ __ __   __ __ __ __ __ __ __ ."

God Is Mighty

Zephaniah 3:17

Zephaniah tells you wonderful things that God will do for you.

Decode this verse and celebrate what you have learned.

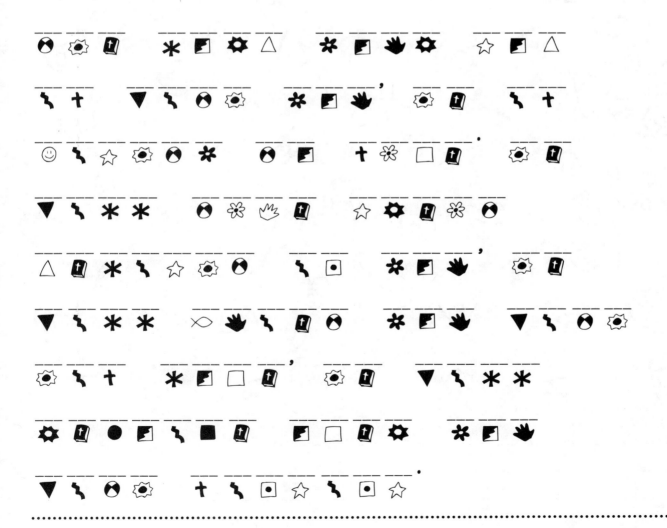

Love

Romans 12:9

When you say you love, do it honestly. Read this verse and use it everyday.

Follow the connected hearts. Write each letter in order on the spaces below.

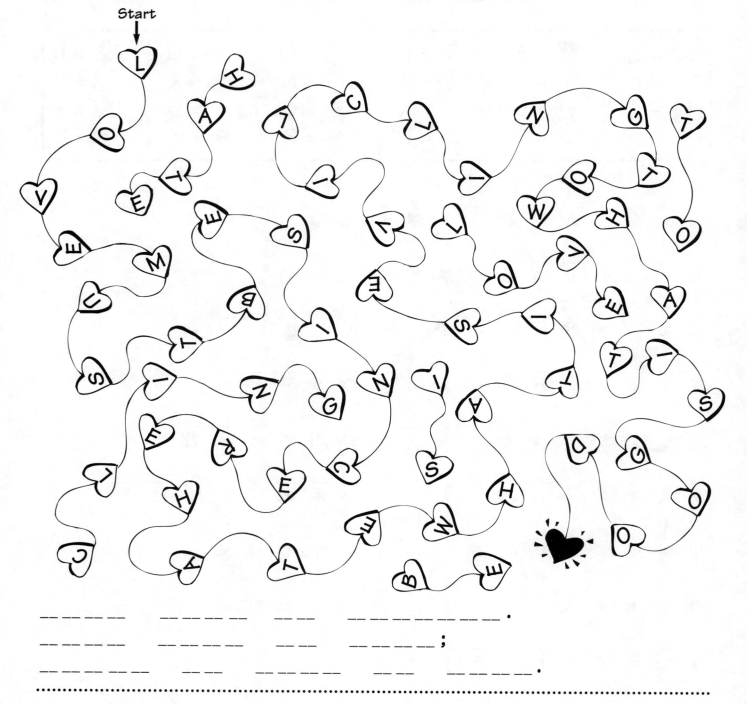

__ __ __ __ __   __ __ __ __   __ __   __ __ __ __ __ __ .

__ __ __ __   __ __ __ __   __ __   __ __ __ __ ;

__ __ __ __ __   __ __   __ __ __ __   __ __ __   __ __ __ __ .

Trust Jesus

Philippians 4:13

When you trust Jesus, Paul tells us that you can do anything because God will give you the strength you need.

Use the Braille alphabet to decode this verse.

Love One Another

John 13:34

Jesus gave us a new commandment. Think about how much God loves you and about how much God loves everyone.

Use the key to decode the verse.

Key:

A = Y	I = R	S = H
C = W	L = O	T = G
D = V	M = N	U = E
E = U	N = M	V = D
G = T	O = L	W = C
H = S	R = I	Y = A

"
Y   M U C   W L N N Y M V
_   _ _ _   _ _ _ _ _ _ _

R   T R D U   A L E :
_   _ _ _ _   _ _ _

O L D U   L M U   Y M L G S U I .
_ _ _ _   _ _ _   _ _ _ _ _ _ _

Y H   R   S Y D U   O L D U V   A L E ,
_ _   _   _ _ _ _   _ _ _ _ _   _ _ _

H L   A L E   N E H G
_ _   _ _ _   _ _ _ _

O L D U   L M U   Y M L G S U I . "
_ _ _ _   _ _ _   _ _ _ _ _ _ _

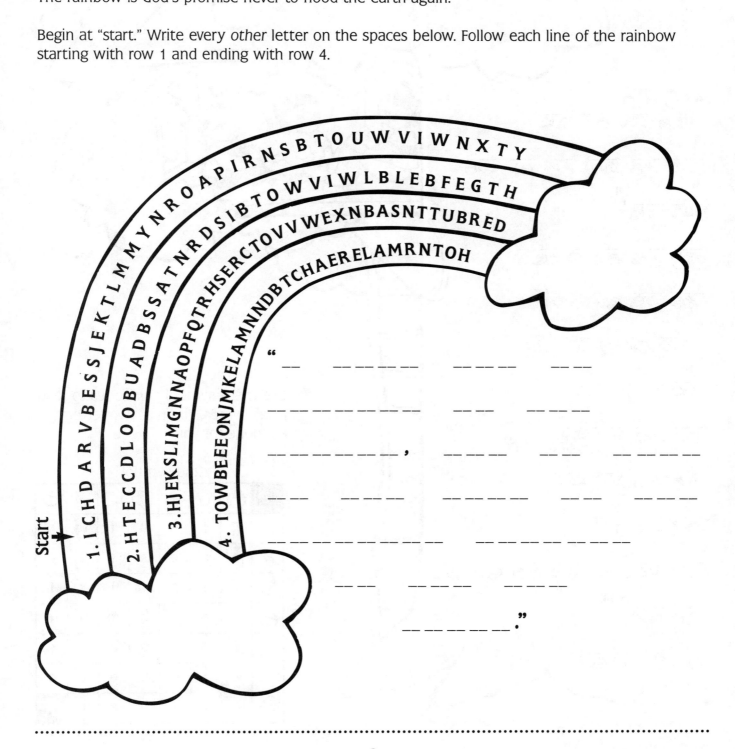

God's Promise

Genesis 9:13

The rainbow is God's promise never to flood the earth again.

Begin at "start." Write every *other* letter on the spaces below. Follow each line of the rainbow starting with row 1 and ending with row 4.

Share Your Faith

Matthew 4:19

Jesus will help you tell your friends all about him.

Use these symbol pair codes to read Jesus' words. The first two letters are done for you.

1st symbol \ 2nd symbol	🔔	🗸	🛶	🌰	🐟	🪱	⚓
⚓	c	f	e	u	l	w	s
🪱	o	o	e	s	i	l	o
🗸	m	l	s	i	l	k	f
🌰	e	o	s	d	m	y	m
🐟	l	m	a	a	a	f	e
🍪	w	j	n	d	e	u	n
🛶	o	i	s	h	e	r	

© Carson Dellosa • CD-2021

10

Memory Verse Mysteries 4–6

The Young Have Faith

1 Timothy 4:12

Even though you are young, you can understand what it means to love Jesus.

This verse will encourage you to set an example for others.

Use the picture symbols to help read this verse of encouragement. Look for the letter that is at the intersection of the two symbols. The first word is done for you.

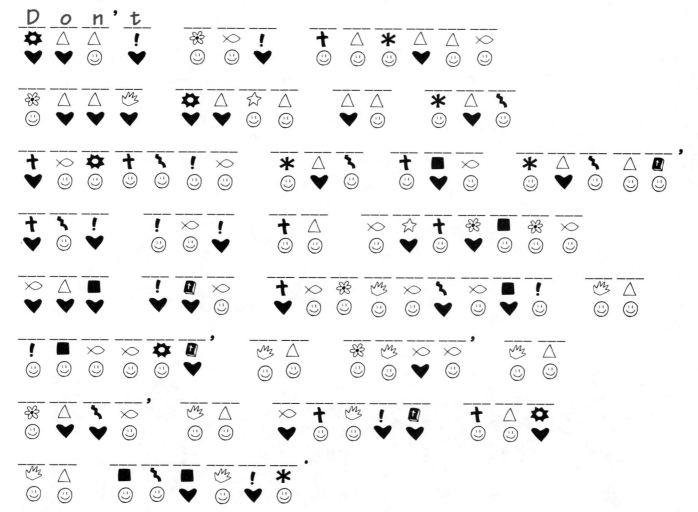

Rejoice!

Philippians 4:4

Rejoice in the Lord always! His love for you is worth celebrating.

Use the megaphone alphabet to find out what this verse says.

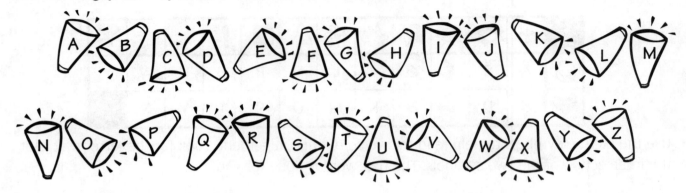

___ ___ ___ ___ ___ ___ ___　　___ ___　　___ ___ ___
T–2 D+1 H+2 P–1 J–1 A+2 H–3　　G+2 M+1　　V–2 E+3 C+2

___ ___ ___ ___　　___ ___ ___ ___ ___ .
N–2 P–1 Q+1 F–2　　C–2 M–1 W–O B–1 W+2 T–1

___　　___ ___ ___ ___　　___ ___ ___
H+1　　T+3 J–1 N–2 K+1　　T–1 C–2 X+1

___ ___　　___ ___ ___ ___ ___ :
K–2 U–1　　C–2 F+1 B–1 J–1 P–2

___ ___ ___ ___ ___ ___ ___ !
S–1 C+2 L–2 P–1 H+1 D–1 B+3

What Is Faith?

Hebrews 11:1

Faith is something you cannot see; you know it is true and it gives you hope.

Replace the letter in the code with the letter just to the right of it in the alphabet.

A B C D E F G H I J K L M N O P Q R S T U V W X Y Z

M N V   E Z H S G

H R   A D H M F   R T Q D

N E   V G Z S   V D

G N O D   E N Q   Z M C

B D Q S Z H M   N E

V G Z S   V D   C N

M N S   R D D .

Treat Everyone Like Jesus

Matthew 25:40

Jesus said that whatever you do for anyone, you have also done it for him. We can do good to other people as if we are doing good to Jesus.

Use this code to read what Jesus said.

•| = A	= = D	•_ = G	\\\\ = J	•\ = M	|• = P	÷ = S	•• = V
// = B	⁻• = E	•| = H	•// = K	•\\ = N	| = Q	≐ = T	= = W
•|• = C	% = F	∧ = I	//• = L	\\• = O	//• = R	•• = U	= = Y

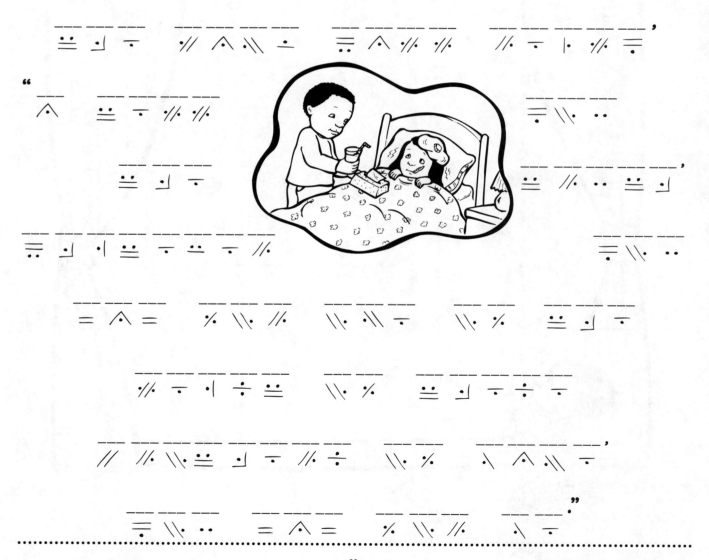

© Carson-Dellosa CD-2021

Trust God

Proverbs 3:5–6

When you trust God with all your heart, God will guide your life.

Color in only the boxes with a ● and ■. The remaining boxes will reveal this verse.

I	F	T	R	U	S	T	A	L	L	I	N	A	T	L	T	H	E	T	O
R	L	O	R	D	R	U	W	W	I	T	H	H	A	L	L	L	O	V	E
S	T	O	P	T	Y	O	U	R	P	E	O	P	L	E	W	H	O	T	O
M	E	W	A	R	O	P	E	O	H	E	A	R	T	U	P	A	N	D	T
L	E	A	N	H	O	W	N	O	T	Y	O	U	O	N	A	M	O	N	G
T	O	Y	O	U	R	P	O	O	R	O	W	N	P	A	T	I	E	N	C
A	L	L	G	U	N	D	E	R	S	T	A	N	D	I	N	G	;	T	O
I	N	N	O	A	L	L	M	Y	O	U	R	U	S	W	A	Y	S	B	R
T	O	A	C	K	N	O	W	L	E	D	G	E	T	A	L	H	I	M	,
L	O	V	A	N	D	A	N	H	E	H	E	W	I	L	L	L	O	V	E
L	M	A	K	E	H	O	P	E	S	Y	O	U	R	L	O	V	E	T	O
E	H	T	P	A	T	H	S	S	S	T	R	A	I	G	H	T	.	A	L

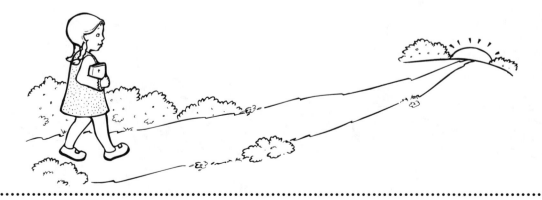

God Protects

Psalm 91:11–12

This Psalm promises you that God will always be where you are, protecting you.

Look at the stones with letters on this page. Discover the verse by writing the letter of the stone that is two stones to the left of the one written under the lines.

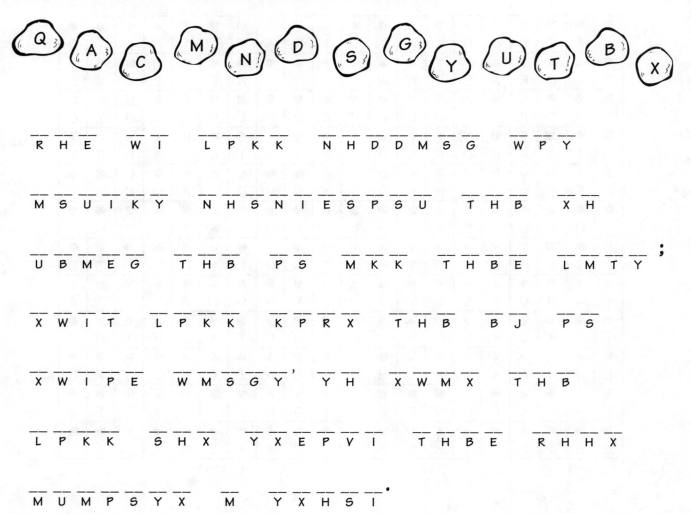

R H E   W I   L P K K   N H D D M S G   W P Y

M S U I K Y   N H S N I E S P S U   T H B   X H

U B M E G   T H B   P S   M K K   T H B E   L M T Y ;

X W I T   L P K K   K P R X   T H B   B J   P S

X W I P E   W M S G Y '   Y H   X W M X   T H B

L P K K   S H X   Y X E P V I   T H B E   R H H X

M U M P S Y X   M   Y X H S I .

Fruit of the Spirit

Galatians 5:22–23

This verse tells us about the fruit of God's Spirit. These "fruit" are our character traits and behaviors that show we belong to God.

Use this grid to decode the verse. Practice what you read.

But the fruit of the Spirit is

Lift Your Eyes

Psalm 121:1–2

Lifting your eyes to the Lord means to go to God in prayer. The Lord is ready to help you. All you need to do is ask.

Read this verse of praise by matching the numbers to the correct letters.

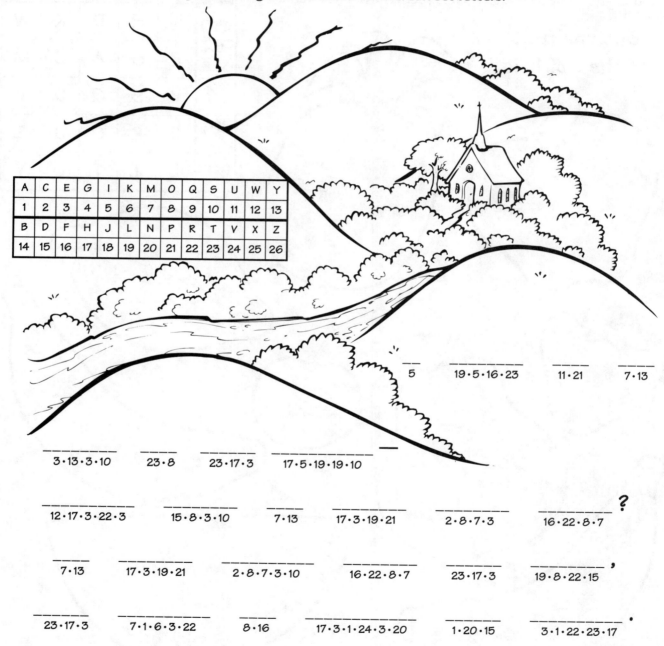

A	C	E	G	I	K	M	O	Q	S	U	W	Y
1	2	3	4	5	6	7	8	9	10	11	12	13
B	D	F	H	J	L	N	P	R	T	V	X	Z
14	15	16	17	18	19	20	21	22	23	24	25	26

___   _____   _____   ____
5   19·5·16·23   11·21   7·13

_____   _____   _____   _____
3·13·3·10   23·8   23·17·3   17·5·19·19·10

_____   _____   ____   _____   _____   _____ **?**
12·17·3·22·3   15·8·3·10   7·13   17·3·19·21   2·8·7·3   16·22·8·7

____   _____   _____   _____   _____   _____ **,**
7·13   17·3·19·21   2·8·7·3·10   16·22·8·7   23·17·3   19·8·22·15

_____   _____   ____   _____   _____   _____ **.**
23·17·3   7·1·6·3·22   8·16   17·3·1·24·3·20   1·20·15   3·1·22·23·17

        Memory Verse Mysteries 4–6

I Am the Way

John 14:6

There is only one way to know God. Do you know the way?

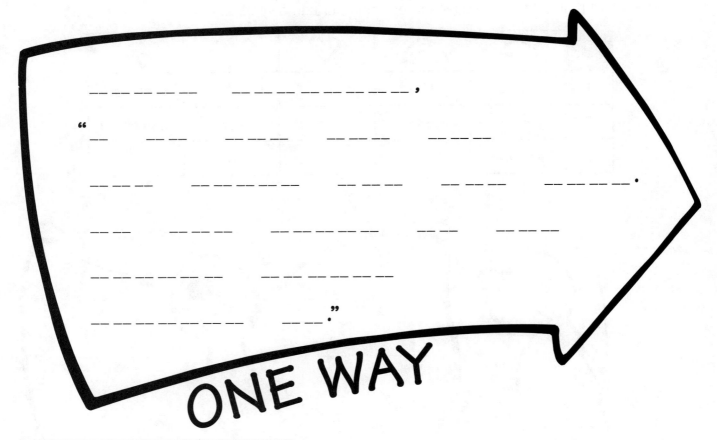

ONE WAY

Begin with the first letter on the grid and write every other letter in order on the space above. You will need to go through the grid twice, and you will use every letter.

♥	J	I	E	F	S	E	U	N
S	O	A	O	N	N	S	E	W
C	E	O	R	M	E	E	D	S
I	T	A	O	M	T	T	H	H
E	E	F	W	A	A	T	Y	H
A	E	N	R	D	E	T	X	H
C	E	E	T	P	R	T	U	T
T	H	H	R	A	O	N	U	D
G	T	H	H	M	E	E	L	♥

A New Creation

2 Corinthians 5:17

Once you know Jesus' love in your heart, he will make you new in him!

Find the word that is at the intersection of a number and a symbol. Write it on the correct line.

	🐟	🌈	♥	☀	⛵
1	come	the	in	if	creation
2	new	is	he	old	therefore
3	anyone	Christ	gone	a	has

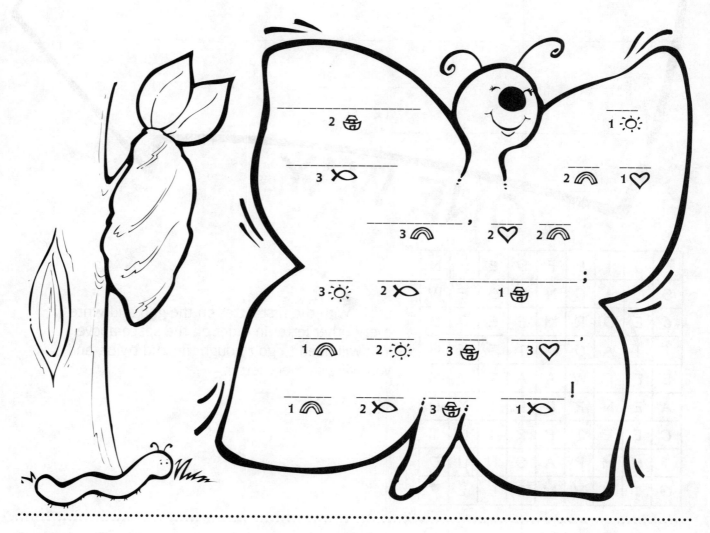

God's Love

Romans 8:38–39

Nothing can ever come between you and all the love Jesus has for you.

Can you decode this Bible verse?

_____ _ ___ _____ ____
ROF   I   MA   DECNIVNOC   TAHT

_____ _____ ___ ____ ,
REHTIEN   HTAED   RON   EFIL

_____ _____ ___ _____ , _____ ___
REHTIEN   SLEGNA   RON   SNOMED   REHTIEN   EHT

_____ ___ ___ _____ ,
TNESERP   RON   EHT   ERUTUF

___ ___ _____ , _____ _____
RON   YNA   SREWOP   REHTIEN   THGIEH

___ _____ , ___ _____ ____
RON   HTPED   RON   GNIHTYNA   ESLE

__ ___ _____ , ____ __ ____
NI   LLA   NOITAERC   LLIW   EB   ELBA

__ _____ __ ____ ___ ____
OT   ETARAPES   SU   MORF   EHT   EVOL

__ ___ ____ __ __
FO   DOG   TAHT   SI   NI

_____ _____ ___ _____ .
TSIRHC   SUSEJ   RUO   DROL

Hint: All words are written backwards.

A Place for You

John 14:2

Jesus says that we will always be with him in a place made especially for each of us.

Use the alphabet code below to read just what Jesus said.

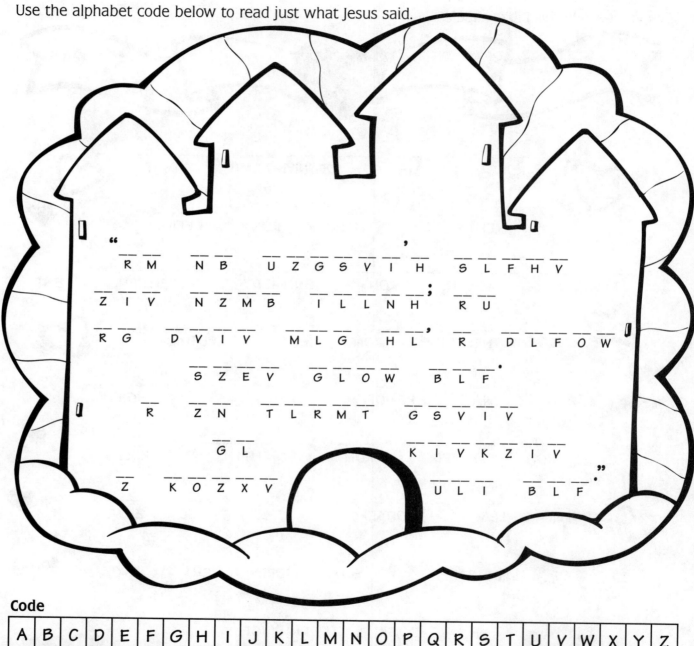

Code

A	B	C	D	E	F	G	H	I	J	K	L	M	N	O	P	Q	R	S	T	U	V	W	X	Y	Z
Z	Y	X	W	V	U	T	S	R	Q	P	O	N	M	L	K	J	I	H	G	F	E	D	C	B	A

Meaning

Memory Verse Mysteries 4–6

God's Word

Psalm 119:105

The Bible is God's word. Read it every day to help guide your heart and actions.

Write in the letter that comes just *after* the letter written to read this verse. Use A for Z.

X N T Q   V N Q C

H R   Z   K Z L O

S N   L X   E D D S

Z M C   Z   K H F G S

E N Q   L X   O Z S G.

Believe

Romans 10:9

Paul tells us that salvation comes from believing in God's power and confessing that Jesus is Lord of your life.

Finish the verse by filling in the missing vowels. (If you need help, use the code.)

Code:

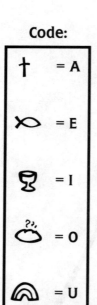

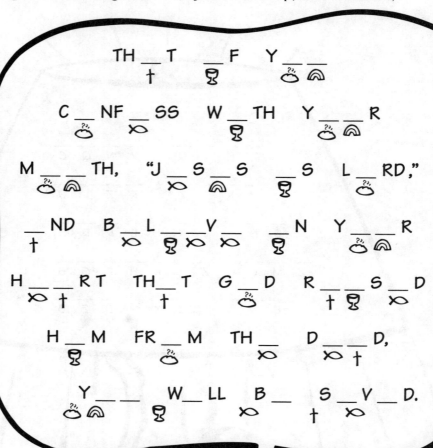

Name _____

God Is Always with You

Joshua 1:9

With this verse, God promises always to be with you. Just as God guided Joshua, God will give you courage.

Use the code below to read the verse.

Code

8	10	12	3	4	1	2	5	6	20	19	13	11	9	7	17	26	25	21	24	16	23	14	15	22	18
A	B	C	D	E	F	G	H	I	J	K	L	M	N	O	P	Q	R	S	T	U	V	W	X	Y	Z

Meaning

" 5 8 23 4   6   9 7 24   12 7 11 11 8 9 3 4 3

22 7 16 **?**   10 4   21 24 25 7 9 2   8 9 3

12 7 16 25 8 2 4 7 16 21 **.**   3 7   9 7 24   10 4

24 4 25 25 6 1 6 4 3 **;**   3 7   9 7 24   10 4

3 6 21 12 7 16 25 8 2 4 3 **,**   1 7 25   24 5 4

13 7 25 3   22 7 16 25   2 7 3   14 6 13 13   10 4

14 6 24 5   22 7 16   14 5 4 25 4 23 4 25   22 7 16 **.** "

25

Jesus Called You

Romans 1:6

Did you know that Jesus has called you to belong to him and follow his ways?

Memorize this verse after you decode it. Do your math correctly to read this verse.

$$
\begin{array}{ccc}
\underline{}\ \underline{}\ \underline{} & \underline{}\ \underline{}\ \underline{} & \underline{}\ \underline{}\ \underline{}\ \underline{} \\
\begin{array}{ccc} 2 & 19 & 3 \\ +2 & -2 & +4 \end{array} &
\begin{array}{ccc} 11 & 9 & 17 \\ +17 & +9 & +7 \end{array} &
\begin{array}{cccc} 4 & 12 & 18 & 28 \\ -0 & +3 & +4 & -10 \end{array}
\end{array}
$$

$$
\begin{array}{cc}
\begin{array}{ccc} 1 & 11 & 16 \\ +3 & +10 & -8 \end{array} &
\begin{array}{ccccc} 4 & 10 & 10 & 9 & 5 \\ +0 & +6 & +8 & +8 & +5 \end{array}
\end{array}
$$

$$
\begin{array}{cc}
\begin{array}{ccccc} 32 & 13 & 25 & 33 & 15 \\ -9 & -2 & -7 & -11 & -7 \end{array} &
\begin{array}{ccc} 22 & 9 & 12 \\ +4 & +2 & +6 \end{array}
\end{array}
$$

$$
\begin{array}{ccc}
\begin{array}{ccc} 2 & 9 & 16 \\ +2 & +12 & -8 \end{array} &
\begin{array}{cccccc} 11 & 4 & 7 & 25 & 4 & 20 \\ -5 & -0 & +8 & -10 & +4 & -13 \end{array} &
\begin{array}{cc} 15 & 18 \\ +8 & -0 \end{array}
\end{array}
$$

$$
\begin{array}{cccc}
\begin{array}{cccccc} 2 & 12 & 17 & 25 & 9 & 7 \\ +3 & -4 & -2 & -7 & +8 & +3 \end{array} &
\begin{array}{cc} 18 & 20 \\ +5 & -2 \end{array} &
\begin{array}{ccccc} 7 & 10 & 17 & 12 & 30 \\ +6 & -2 & +5 & +12 & -8 \end{array} &
\begin{array}{cccccc} 3 & 10 & 13 & 24 & 11 & 26 \\ +3 & +1 & +8 & -12 & +11 & -3 \end{array}
\end{array}
$$

Code

4	5	6	7	8	9	10	11	12	13	14	15	16	17	18	19	20	21	22	23	24	25	26	27	28	29
A	B	C	D	E	F	G	H	I	J	K	L	M	N	O	P	Q	R	S	T	U	V	W	X	Y	Z

Meaning

Memory Verse Mysteries 4–6

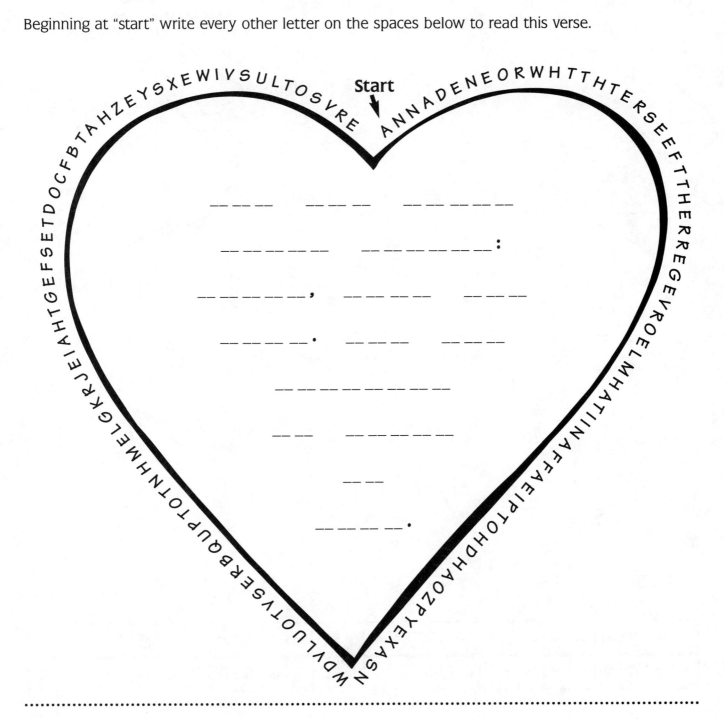

Love Is the Greatest

1 Corinthians 13:13

Paul tells us, as Jesus told him, that there is only one thing that is the greatest. This is an easy verse to memorize.

Beginning at "start" write every other letter on the spaces below to read this verse.

Start

__ __ __ __   __ __ __ __   __ __ __ __ __ __

__ __ __ __ __ __   __ __ __ __ __ __ :

__ __ __ __ __ __ ,   __ __ __ __ __   __ __ __ __

__ __ __ __ __ .   __ __ __ __   __ __ __ __

__ __ __ __ __ __ __ __ __

__ __ __   __ __ __ __ __

__ __ __

__ __ __ __ __ .

Children of the Resurrection

Luke 20:36

All who believe in God's goodness live forever through Jesus. Believe that you are a child of God.

Use the code below to find out how you are like the angels.

A	B	C	D	E	F	G	H	I	J	K	L	M	N	O	P	Q	R	S	T	U	V	W	X	Y	Z

28

God So Loved the World

John 3:16

God loves this world so much that he sent his son to show us how to live and die.

Use this verse to help tell other people about God. The first word is done for you.

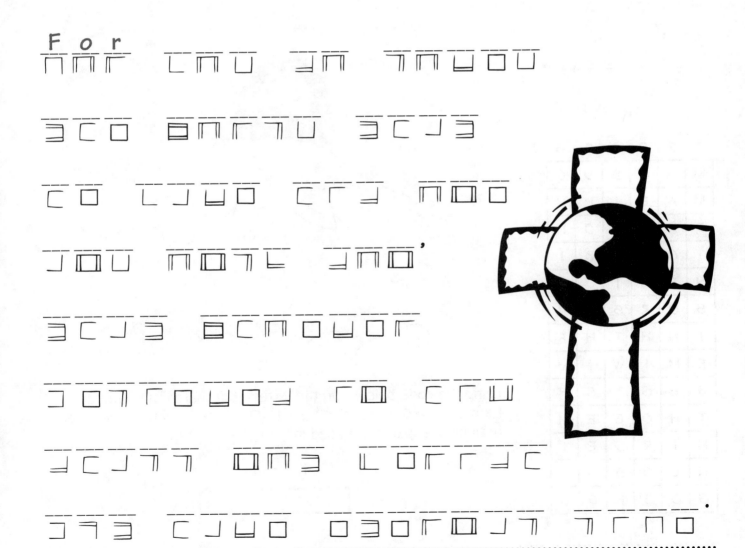

For

Jesus, without Sin

2 Corinthians 5:21

God made Jesus, who was without sin, to die for you so you could be saved.

‗ ‗ ‗   ‗ ‗   ‗ ‗ ‗   ‗ ‗ ‗   ‗ ‗ ‗

‗ ‗   ‗ ‗ ‗   ‗ ‗ ‗   ‗ ‗   ‗ ‗ ‗   ‗ ‗ ‗   ‗ ‗,

‗ ‗   ‗ ‗ ‗ ‗ ‗   ‗ ‗ ‗   ‗ ‗ ‗ ‗

‗ ‗ ‗ ‗ ‗ ‗   ‗ ‗ ‗   ‗ ‗ ‗ ‗   ‗ ‗ ‗ ‗ ‗

‗ ‗ ‗   ‗ ‗ ‗ ‗.

	1	2	3	4	5	6
	M	A	G	D	D	O
	M	W	E	I	H	H
	D	N	O	A	O	H
	T	O	S	N	B	I
	N	F	E	I	O	S
	S	O	R	S	T	U
	I	N	H	T	H	A
	E	M	I	W	I	M
	B	E	G	T	C	H
	T	H	O	E	E	M
	H	T	R	G	E	I
	N	E	O	S	S	U
	G	O	S	F	D	O

Using the code below find the letters that match the numbers. Example: 3 = G, 6 = O, 4 = D, 1 = M. Continue repeating the code until all the spaces are filled in.

The Code:

3	6	4	1	2	5

Praise the Lord

Psalm 150:6

This Psalm says to let everything that breathes praise the Lord–especially you!

Circle the first two letters. Skip one letter. Circle the next two. Skip one. Follow this pattern. Write the circled letters in order at the bottom. The first word is done for you.

Start: L E Q T E Z V E A R Y D T H S I N H G T M H A J T H E A S R B R R E A Y T H
K P R E A I L S E L T H Y E L M O R O D P L R A L I S Y E T M H E C L O N R D

Let _ _ _ _ _ _ _ _ _ _ _ _   _ _ _ _ _

_ _ _ _   _ _ _ _ _ _ _   _ _ _ _ _ _ _

_ _ _ _   _ _ _ _ _ _ .   _ _ _ _ _ _ _ _   _ _ _ _   _ _ _ _ _ .

Memory Verse Mysteries 4–6

Answer Key

Page 4 – John 15:13
"Greater love has no one than this, that he lay down his life for his friends."

Page 5 – Zephaniah 3:17
The Lord your God is with you, he is mighty to save. He will take great delight in you, he will quiet you with his love, he will rejoice over you with singing.

Page 6 – Romans 12:9
Love must be sincere. Hate what is evil; cling to what is good.

Page 7 – Philippians 4:13
I can do everything through him who gives me strength.

Page 8 – John 13:34
"A new command I give you: Love one another. As I have loved you, so you must love one another."

Page 9 – Genesis 9:13
"I have set my rainbow in the clouds, and it will be the sign of the covenant between me and the earth."

Page 10 – Matthew 4:19
"Come follow me," Jesus said, "and I will make you fishers of men."

Page 11 – 1 Timothy 4:12
Don't let anyone look down on you because you are young, but set an example for the believers in speech, in life, in love, in faith and in purity.

Page 12 – Philippians 4:4
Rejoice in the Lord always. I will say it again: Rejoice!

Page 13 – Hebrews 11:1
Now faith is being sure of what we hope for and certain of what we do not see.

Page 14 – Matthew 25:40
The king will reply, "I tell you the truth, whatever you did for one of the least of these brothers of mine, you did for me."

Page 15 – Proverbs 3:5–6
Trust in the LORD with all your heart and lean not on your own understanding; in all your ways acknowledge him, and he will make your paths straight.

Page 16 – Psalm 91:11–12
For he will command his angels concerning you to guard you in all your ways; they will lift you up in their hands, so that you will not strike your foot against a stone.

Page 17 – Galatians 5:22–23
But the fruit of the Spirit is love, joy, peace, patience, kindness, goodness, faithfulness, gentleness and self-control.

Page 18 – Psalm 121:1–2
I lift up my eyes to the hills–where does my help come from? My help comes from the Lord, the maker of heaven and earth.

Page 19 – John 14:6
Jesus answered, "I am the way and the truth and the life. No one comes to the Father except through me."

Page 20 – 2 Corinthians 5:17
Therefore, if anyone is in Christ, he is a new creation; the old has gone, the new has come!

Page 21 – Romans 8:38–39
For I am convinced that neither death nor life, neither angels nor demons, neither the present nor the future, nor any powers, neither height nor depth, nor anything else in all creation, will be able to separate us from the love of God that is in Christ Jesus our Lord.

Page 22 – John 14:2
"In my Father's house are many rooms; if it were not so, I would have told you. I am going there to prepare a place for you."

Page 23 – Psalm 119:105
Your word is a lamp to my feet and a light for my path.

Page 24 – Romans 10:9
That if you confess with your mouth, "Jesus is Lord," and believe in your heart that God raised him from the dead, you will be saved.

Page 25 – Joshua 1:9
"Have I not commanded you? Be strong and courageous. Do not be terrified; do not be discouraged, for the Lord your God will be with you wherever you go."

Page 26 – Romans 1:6
And you also are among those who are called to belong to Jesus Christ.

Page 27 – 1 Corinthians 13:13
And now these three remain: faith, hope and love. But the greatest of these is love.

Page 28 – Luke 20:36
and they can no longer die; for they are like the angels. They are God's children, since they are children of the resurrection.

Page 29 – John 3:16
For God so loved the world that he gave his one and only son, that whoever believes in him shall not perish but have eternal life.

Page 30 – 2 Corinthians 5:21
God made him who had no sin to be sin for us, so that in him we might become the righteousness of God.

Page 31 – Psalm 150:6
Let everything that has breath praise the LORD. Praise the LORD.